AF435524

Overview of the S-Series IPS specifications

ILS-C-2013-002

Issue No. 6.0

IPS Spec Council

This overview has been developed by the following organizations (in alphabetic order):

- AeroSpace and Defence Industries Association of Europe
- Aerospace Industries Association   USA
- Airbus Defense & Space   Germany & Spain
- Boeing   USA
- Dutch MoD   Netherlands
- Isselnord   Italy
- Lockheed Martin   USA
- O'Neil & Associates   USA
- Saab AB   Sweden
- Secondo Mona   Italy
- Team Defence   United Kingdom

The following people contributed to the development of this overview (in alphabetic order):

BESEL, Achim	LUNDQUIST, Joakim
CHIARELLO, Orlando	MEYER, Dawn J
EICHMÜLLER, Peter	MITJANS, Félix
EVANS, André	MRAS, Gery
GYLLSTROM, Leif	MULDER, Gerke
HALPERN, Jamie	SCHIELE, Stefan
HASLAM, Paul	SEIDEL, Bernhard
LAFUENTE RODRÍGUEZ, Jose Carlos	SHOOK, William
GYLLSTROM, Leif	SOMOZA, Ramón
HALPERN, Jamie	TEDESCHI, Stefano
HASLAM, Paul	WILLIAMS, Phil

Copyright

Usage rights 

Publishers

AeroSpace and Defence Industries Association of Europe

Aerospace Industries Association of America (AIA)

Republished 2022 by Editorial Dragón with permission of ASD

ISBN 978-84-19125-02-6

1st edition

Overview of the S-Series IPS specifications

Table of contents

List of tables

List of figures

References

Table 1 References

Chap No./Document No.	Title
www.sx000i.org	The website for all transversal specifications (SX000i, SX001G, SX002D, etc).
www.s1000d.org	The S1000D website
www.s2000m.org	The S2000M website
www.s3000l.org	The S3000L website
www.s4000p.org	The S4000P website
www.s5000f.org	The S5000F website
www.s6000t.org	The S6000T website
www.asd-ste100.org	The ASD-STE100 website

2 The S-Series IPS specifications

Introduction

The international aerospace and defense community have, over the past decades, invested considerable effort to develop specifications in the field of Integrated Product Support (IPS).

The work was initially accomplished by integrated Working Groups (WG) composed of members of the AeroSpace and Defence Industries Association of Europe (ASD) and customer organizations (Ministries of Defence) in a collaborative environment. The structure and functional coverage of these specifications was largely determined by NATO requirements specified in 1993 during an international workshop (HAW Acquisition Logistics) in Paris.

In July 2010, a MoU was signed between ASD and AIA (Aerospace Industries Association of America, Inc.) in order to promote a common suite of Integrated Logistics Support (ILS) specifications for the aerospace and defense industries of Europe and the USA. In order to make optimal use of the resources available, ASD and AIA agreed to work in concert on the joint development of the **former ASD specifications**.

An ILS Specification Council (**now IPS Spec Council**) was formed as a consequence of that MoU in order to provide the overall governance of the development of the **S-Series IPS specifications** except

- S1000D, which is covered under a separate agreement between ASD, AIA and ATA (Air Transport Association of America, Inc.)
- ASD-STE100, which is a purely ASD specification

The IPS Spec Council is therefore the governing body for all the different groups that perform the actual development of the S-Series IPS specifications, with the two exceptions mentioned above. Refer to Fig 1.

In 2019, the new term Integrated Product Support (IPS) replaced the legacy term ILS so as to highlight the fact that the S-Series IPS specifications cover a far wider scope than the traditional ILS. The full suite of specifications is hence called **S-Series IPS specifications**.

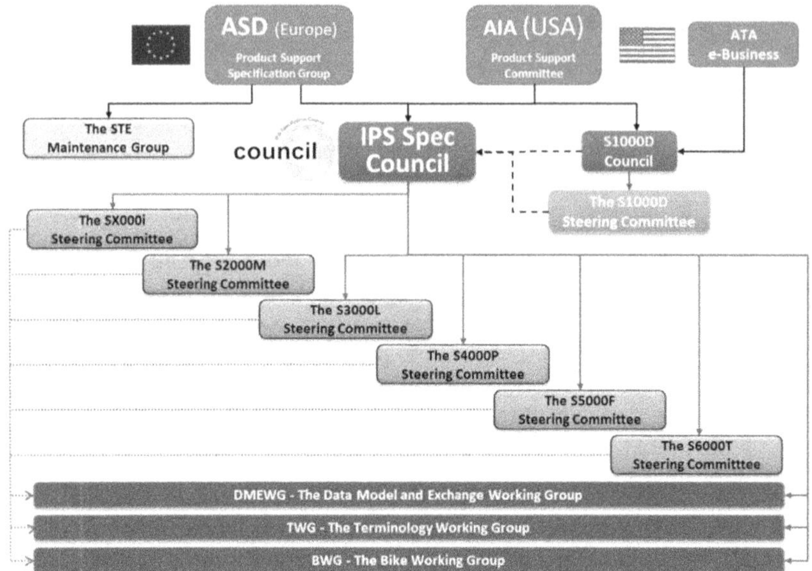

ICN-B6865-IPS202001001-002-01

Fig 1 The organization

At the same time, it was agreed to further ensure the interoperability of the **S-Series IPS specifications** by publishing all together in a so-called "block release". The first block release was made in April 2021 for all specifications except S1000D and ASD-STE100, which fall outside the scope of the IPS Spec Council for the reasons mentioned above.

O'Neil & Associates, Inc. (AIA) provide the services of Editor-in-Chief and are the publishers of the S-Series IPS specifications, with the exception of ASD-STE100.

Vision

The IPS Spec Council's vision for the **S-Series IPS specifications** is to establish an integrated suite of product support specifications for both military and civil products and platforms.

Mission

The mission for the IPS Spec Council, its specification Steering Committees (SC), Working Groups (WG) and Task Teams (TT) is

- to minimize project dependency by defining clear guidance and by managing and limiting inclusion of project and national specific rules and constructs
- to ensure commonality between the IPS related specifications to support the re-use of data across projects
- to give rules and guidelines for the realization of integrated product support and to integrate the different IPS elements (the "I" in IPS is the main driver)
- to ensure the application of the basic ISO standards such as ISO dates and language codes
- to establish well defined data transfer mechanisms between the different logistics disciplines based on internationally accepted and adopted data exchange standards and specifications
- to cover all aspects of supportability over the entire life cycle of a product
- to be the contractual baseline for industry and customers
- to be up to date with the technical development and changes in support philosophy

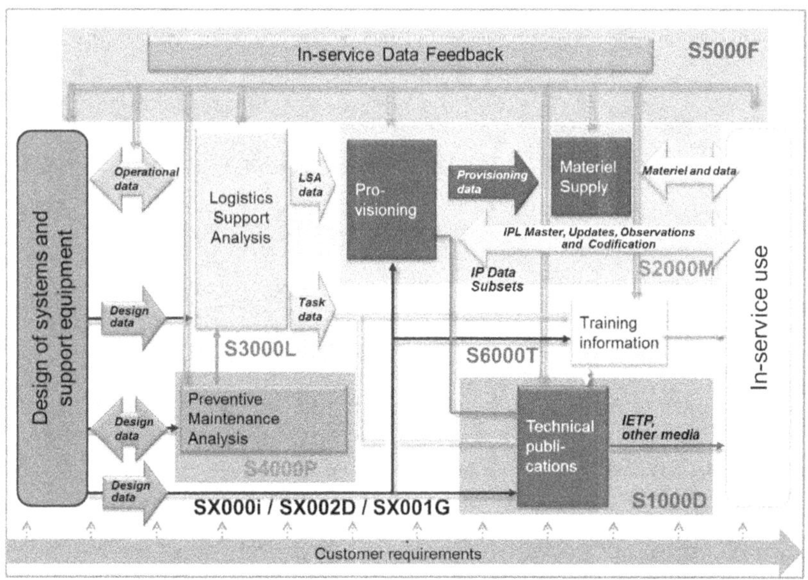

ICN-B6865-SX000I30019-005-01

Fig 2 The S-Series IPS specifications

The following specifications are currently available or in the process of development:

- SX000H – Harmonized Suite of the S-Series Integrated Product Support (IPS) Specifications
- SX000i - International specification for integrated product support (IPS)
- S1000D® – International specification for technical publications using a common source database
- S2000M – International specification for material management – Integrated data processing
- S3000L – International specification for Logistics Support Analysis – LSA
- S4000P – International specification for developing and continuously improving preventive maintenance
- S5000F – International specification for in-service data feedback
- S6000T – International specification for training analysis and design
- SX001G – Glossary for the S-Series IPS specifications
- SX002D – Common data model for the S-Series IPS specifications
- SX004G – Unified Modeling Language (UML) model reader's guidance
- SX005G – S-Series IPS specifications XML schema implementation guidance
- SX006R – S-Series IPS specifications rules definition guide
- S1000X, S2000X, S3000X, S4000X, S6000X – Input data specifications
- ASD-STE100® – Simplified Technical English

Block releases

A lot of work has taken place in recent years to ensure the harmonization and full interoperability of the S-Series IPS specifications and their associated data. As part of this effort, the IPS Spec Council decided to publish all the specifications at the same time, so as to ensure that projects could select a single set of consistent specifications as their contractual baseline.

Block releases will take place every two years, starting on the 30th of April 2021.

3   SX000H – Handbook for the S-Series Integrated Product Support (IPS) Specifications

Introduction

SX000H can be considered as a handbook for reference when the purpose is to (not an exhaustive list):

- implement the S-Series IPS specifications
- combine familiarity with one or more of the S-Series IPS specifications with their integration
- interest in the subject in general

Purpose

SX000H is not a specification, despite the "S" as the first character of its number, as there is no content with which a project must be compliant. Its aim is to describe how data from a design phase to an output phase that produces three distinct outputs, which are S1000D data modules containing:

- a simple maintenance procedure
- an IPD data module
- a learning data module that holds the output from S6000T

SX000H development history

In their early days, some of the S-Series IPS specifications contained a chapter that explained the relationship between one specification and the others. It was recognized that, if this approach was taken, these chapters, and therefore the specifications would become misaligned. The solution to this was the beginning of the development of the "Sn000X" specifications, which are the data input requirements for each of the core specifications.

During an IPS Spec Council meeting, one of the Council Officers gave a briefing on the promotion of adoption of the S-Series IPS specifications, part of which included statements about the S-Series IPS specifications being the first truly integrated suite of product support specifications. If this was true, the brief went on, then it was recommended that the release to the public should be harmonized by issuing all the S-Series IPS specifications on the same date, in an integrated manner.

At subsequent IPS Spec Council meetings, the development of an overarching specification that harmonized the S-Series IPS specifications was approved and that led to the birth of an SC000H (where "C" = "Combined" and "H" = "Harmonized"). As the document was being developed, the decision was made that the "C" wasn't very meaningful and that the document should belong to the SX000i family, since it applied to all the S-Series IPS specifications. As the drafting of SX000H's content was maturing, the use of the word "Harmonized" in the definition of the "H" was replaced with "Handbook" was much more appropriate.

Hence "SX000H - Handbook for the S-Series Integrated Product Support (IPS) Specifications", was borne.

The companies and organizations that have contributed to the development of SX000H are:

–	Airbus	Germany & Spain
–	O'Neil & Associates, Inc.	USA
–	mobiWebcom	USA
–	Team Defence UK	UK

SH000i Issue 1.0 was published in April 2021 as part of the 2021 S-Series IPS specifications block release.

Ten liner

SX000H provides an example of a digital thread for the global IPS process that allows the reader to understand the basic philosophy that allows all S-Series IPS specifications to interact with each other.

SX000H consists of 3 chapters:

- Chapter 1 - Introduction and background
- Chapter 2 - Digital Thread
(2.1 thru 2.4) A description of a digital thread, associated IPS elements and a description of how the S-Series IPS specifications supports this digital thread

- Chapter 3 - Examples of data flow, including
  - Design data and S4000P
  - S4000P data and S3000L
  - S3000L activities
  - S3000L data and S2000M
  - S3000L and S1000D

- S3000L and S6000T
- S2000M and S1000D

4 SX000i - International specification for integrated product support (IPS)

Introduction

By defining common support processes to be used across all S-Series IPS specifications and the interactions of the current S-Series IPS specifications with the different support processes, the SX000i forms the basis for sharing and exchanging data securely through the life of products and services. It provides the key processes and information that allow an IPS program to be launched and sustained.

Purpose

SX000i provides a global IPS reference process, a guide for the use of the S-Series IPS specifications and an overall IPS program guidance for product support managers and practitioners. It also provides the necessary data model and XML schemas in order to exchange IPS-level information between all affected actors.

SX000i:

- explains the vision and objectives for the suite of **S-Series IPS specifications**
- provides a framework that documents the global IPS process and interactions
- explains how the S-Series IPS specifications interface with other standardization domains including program management, global supply chain management, engineering, manufacturing, security, safety, configuration management, quality, data exchange and integration, and life cycle cost
- provides guidance on how to satisfy specific business requirements using an appropriate selection of defined processes and specifications
- defines the IPS data and information to be exchanged with other stakeholders and lower-level processes,
- outlines how to carry out an IPS program across the whole product lifecycle, and provides instructions on how to tailor SX000i and how to contract against it

SX000i development history

During the development of the S-Series IPS specifications, the different SCs and WGs identified the need for an "umbrella" specification to ensure the compatibility and commonality of IPS processes among the S-Series IPS specifications. In 2011, the decision was made to develop, publicize and maintain an Integrated Logistics Support Guide, named SX000i, so as to provide a compatible and common IPS process to be used in the other S-Series IPS specifications. Development of SX000i was viewed by the IPS Specifications Council as an essential step to achieve the vision for the S-Series IPS specifications.

In June of 2011, the SX000i working group was formed and SX000i development started. A first issue was published in December 2015 as SX000i, *International guide for the use of the S-Series of Integrated Logistics Support (ILS) specifications*, with successive issues in July 2016 and December 2018. The specification governance chapter (Chap 4) was removed in Issue 1.2 and converted into a separate document, *IPS-C-2020-010-001*, under the direct control of the IPS Specifications Council.

Issue 2 was published in March 2020. The current title of SX000i, *International specification for Integrated Product Support (IPS)*, was approved by the IPS Spec Council in April 2019.

Issue 3 was published in April 2021 as part of the 2021 S-Series IPS specifications block release.

Following the creation of the SX000i SC, the Data Model and Exchange Working Group (DMEWG) was formed under the ILS Specifications Council (now IPS Specifications Council) in October 2011. Working in close cooperation with the SX000i WG, the DMEWG coordinates the data modeling activities that are performed within the respective S-Series IPS specifications SCs and WGs so as to harmonize and consolidate data requirements into one coherent data model. Thus, SX000i data can flow into the different S-Series IPS specifications in an integrated manner.

Publication of SX000i, and continuing DMEWG coordination activities, enable the achievement of the vision for the suite of IPS specifications "to apply common logistics processes so as to share and exchange data securely through the life of products and services".

The companies and organizations that are currently contributing to the development of SX000i are:

– Airbus DS	Germany and Spain
– Aspire Consulting Limited	UK
– Boeing Defence Systems	USA
– Bundeswehr	Germany
– CDS Defence & Security	UK
– Department of National Defence	Canada
– ESG	Germany
– FACC AG	Austria
– HEME GmbH	Germany
– Leonardo	Italy
– O'Neil & Associates, Inc.	USA
– Schiebel	Austria
– Saab	Sweden
– SELEX ES	Italy
– Thales Group	Netherlands
– UK MoD	UK

The following issues of SX000i have been published:

- SX000i Issue 1.0: December 2015
- SX000i Issue 1.1: July 2016
- SX000i Issue 1.2: December 2018
- SX000i issue 2.0: March 2020.
- SX000i Issue 3.0: April 2021 (part of 2021 S-Series IPS specifications block release)

Ten-liner

SX000i provides the framework for the global IPS process, as well as the guidelines for the selection and use of the respective S-Series IPS specifications. It also provides guidance for the implementation of an IPS program, including tailoring of the specification itself and how to contract against it. Finally, it allows to exchange IPS-level information between all affected parties.

SX000i consists of 11 chapters, which can be grouped as follows:

- Chapter 1   Introduction to the specification
- Chapter 2   IPS framework
- Chapters 4-7   IPS program guidance
- Chapter 8   Tailoring and contracting
- Chapters 9-10   Data model, including UML model, class definitions, data elements and valid values
- Chapters 11-12   Terminology and comparison with that of other specifications

Website

Free download is available at www.sx000i.org

5   S1000D® - International specification for technical publications using a common source database

Introduction

S1000D® (European Community Registered Trade Mark) is an international specification that gives rules and guidance for the production of technical publications, using XML and storing the information as "data modules" in a Common Source Database (CSDB). Data modules are small XML files that typically contain, for example, a single maintenance procedure.

Purpose

This specification is predicated on the concept of "write once, use many", using data modules which can be reused and/or repurposed in one or many ways. Structural integrity and consistency is supported by 30 XML Schemas for different types of information.

S1000D development history

S1000D was born from a need to support a multi-nation, multi-manufacturer aerospace project known as European Combat Aircraft (ECA). The need was realized by project leads who observed that the technical publications from the nations and manufacturers were being written to different specifications, which led to inconsistencies. In 1985 this situation prompted the Documentation working group of ASD (formerly AECMA) to invite military representatives from the European nations to form a joint team for the development of a common military aircraft specification for technical publications.

Release history:

1989

The first issue of the specification was released at the Paris airshow in June 1989. During the following years, five changes (Change 1.1 thru Change 1.5) were released.

1995

The first "full blown" specification (Change 1.6) was published in 1995 and consisted of four main chapters in two volumes with 24 Annexes and one SGML Document Type Definition (DTD). The specification provided for descriptive, procedural and general information for air vehicles, engines and aerospace ground equipment. Interactive Electronic Technical Publications (IETP) were linear, database oriented or integrated and supported by HyTime.

1998

The next issue of S1000D was Change 1.7 which was released in 1998. There was a significant change in this issue from Change 1.6. Aerospace ground equipment was supported by separate DTDs for descriptive, procedural and schedules information. Air vehicles were supported by these plus crew and illustrated parts information. SGML DTDs were also provided for data dispatch notes, In-Process review forms and CSDB lists. The concept of Web based IETPs was also introduced in this issue.

1999

In 1999, Change 1.8 of the specification was released. In the main, Change 1.8 harmonized the aerospace ground equipment DTDs and the air vehicle, engine and equipment DTDs.

2001

Change 1.9 was released in 2001. The most significant aspects of Change 1.9 were the introduction of XML DTDs and IETP-X, which used XML based functionality such as XLink. Also included in this change was relaxation of the rules for the use of different file types to allow for types such as PNG and PDF, and the removal of various elements that were presentation related.

2003

In 2003, at Issue 2.0, S1000D was transformed and completely restructured into nine main chapters that now supported not only air vehicles, engines and aerospace ground equipment but also land and sea based defense projects. It was at this issue that a MoU was signed between ASD and the AIA to jointly maintain future issues of the specification. Another significant change was the introduction of XML Schemas. More information types – commenting, data module lists and publication modules were also added to the suite of SGML and XML DTDs and XML Schemas. This was also the issue that introduced the Process data module and the functionality matrix.

2004

Issue 2.1 was released in 2004. The changes were mainly editorial but more importantly, the new SGML DTDs and XML

Schemas were added to support wiring data modules. Also in 2004, a MoU was signed between ASD and Advanced Distributed Learning (ADL) with the intention to harmonize the requirements of Sharable Content Object Reference Model (SCORM) with S1000D.

2005

2005, at Issue 2.2, the Business Rules EXchange (BREX) data module was introduced and a large number of change proposals were resolved.

2007

In 2007, a MoU was signed between ASD, AIA and ATA and Issue 2.3 was released. Important changes at this issue were the introduction of the Technical Information Repository (TIR), the container concept and the beginnings of a new applicability model. At Issue 2.3, the concept of the "Product" was introduced and XML was declared as the master text format as opposed to SGML.

Later in 2007 Issue 3.0 was released. This issue included important changes to the wiring DTDs and XML Schemas but of most significance was the enhancement of the applicability model, which finally replaced the applicability model that was there in S1000D since Change 1.6.

2008

In 2008, S1000D was completely revised again and now included over 100 change proposals, including the introduction of the new checklist XML Schema and support for the Maintenance Allocation Chart (MAC). Issue 4.0 also included the first results of the harmonization with SCORM and learning and SCORM content package Schemas were introduced. The container and TIR functionality was further enhanced.

The support of SGML was finally dropped at Issue 4.0.

2009

In 2009, Issue 4.0.1 was released as a complete replacement of Issue 4.0 to fix deficiencies experienced when applying Issue 4.0.

2012

In 2012, Issue 4.1 was released. This issue included more restructuring, a large amount of editorial changes plus bringing the specification up to date in many areas. The TIR became a Common Information Repository (CIR) because it now supports externalized applicability annotations as well as a centralized warning and caution repository. The concept of incremental updates of CIR data modules was also included together with the introduction of a new data module type, the update file. The harmonization with SCORM was significantly enhanced to include a new XML Schema for the Sharable Content Object (SCO), and the assessment functionality was improved upon. New XML Schemas were also introduced to support service bulletins and front matter. A new business rules index was added to assist readers in locating business rule decision points for adapting S1000D to project and/or organizational needs.

2016

End of 2016 the latest Issue 4.2 was released. Two new schemas were introduced to support the generation of a Business Rules (BR) document data module and to allow Information Control Number (ICN) metadata file generation which contains metadata related to ICN objects. In addition several updates were included in the area of Applicability/Layout, Business Rules, Common Information Repository, Graphics, Illustrated Parts Data, Layout, Learning, Maintenance Task Data, References and Security. Finally other changes (some cleanup, some updates for Service Bulletin and Standard Numbering System) were included.

2019

In 2019, the latest Issue 5.0 was released. In this issue corrections and updates in the perimeter of Business Rules, Applicability, InfoName/InfoCode, Standard Numbering System (SNS), Illustrated Parts Data (IPD) Schema, Regulatory Information Identification and other updates to satisfy relevant business needs were incorporated. Furthermore some editorial cleanup was implemented.

Ten-liner

- S1000D provides W3C compliant XML Schemas for all information types that are found in technical publications
- The specification describes in detail the purpose and associated rules for every XML element and attribute that is given in the XML Schemas

- Consistency is assured by a rigid metadata structure that is included in every data module
- The processes for using this metadata to manage the information in the CSDB is fully detailed
- XML Schemas are also provided to support the exchange of information
- Publication modules serve as a means to assemble all relevant data modules and associated graphics and multimedia objects into a publication
- Publication modules are the building blocks of a publication and further enhance the reuse and repurposing of data modules and associated graphics and multimedia objects
- Rules and guidance are provided for all output types such as the layout for paper, the presentation of page oriented publications and display and functionality of IETPs
- The technical concepts and rules pertaining to the use of XML are fully explained
- To assist implementations in different projects, business rules, the BREX data module and the business rules index are provided.

Website

Free download is available at www.s1000d.org

Page intentionally blank

6   S2000M - International specification for material management - Integrated data processing

Introduction

The specification S2000M defines the processes, procedures and provides the information for data exchange to be used for material management throughout the lifecycle of a product.

Purpose

The specification standardizes the business relationship between two or more parties (eg, contractor and customer) by providing a well-defined process flow and associated relevant transactions for data exchange.

Chapter 1 Provisioning

Provisioning is the process of selecting support items and spares, necessary for the support of all categories of Products. This chapter defines the process and specifies the data, formats and transmission procedures to be used in providing provisioning information to the customer throughout the various phases of the lifecycle of the Product. It also provides the data set from which Illustrated Parts Catalogues (IPC) are produced. The rules for the production and presentation of the IPC in different media are covered by the specification S1000D. IPC is identical to Illustrated Parts Data Publication (IPDP).

Chapter 1-1 Provisioning General; covers the presentation of a baseline for a Product, the presentation of its data as well as the update of that presentation.

Chapter 1-2 Observations; defines the exchange of information between customer and contractor, or vice versa, during the Provisioning Process; they are typically based on review by either party of the Provisioning Data or updates thereof.

Chapter 1-3 Codification; covers the NATO codification processes and information flows between industry, the National Codification Bureau (NCB) and the customer for all activities related to codification. However, S2000M can be applied without using NATO codification.

Chapter 2 Spare Parts List

The Spare Parts List allows the customer and contractor to process parts data (including commercial data) to allow for the processes as described in chapter 3 of this specification, without the necessity to use processes as described in chapter 1 of this specification.

Chapter 3 Material Supply
This chapter describes the process, the procedures and techniques for on-line operation of pricing, ordering, shipment and invoicing

Chapter 3-1 Material supply general; provides processes, procedures and techniques for pricing, order administration, transportation and invoicing.

Pricing includes processes, procedures and techniques for requesting quotations and providing prices using three different methods:

- single prices
- price lists
- order-based prices.

Pricing supports the alternatives of the establishment of direct binding prices as well as the involvement of a price approval authority. Pricing also supports mutual supply support.

Order administration provides processes, procedures and techniques for placement of orders, order progression and delivery of ordered items. It also supports the administration of orders for services eg, repair.

Transportation provides processes, procedures and techniques for generating and forwarding transport related information.

Invoicing provides processes, procedures and techniques for generating and forwarding invoices as well as for the invoice acceptance or invoice rejection.

Chapter 3-2 Material Supply Data Exchange; provides processes, procedures and techniques for placement of orders, order progression and delivery of ordered items. It supports the administration of orders for items as well as for services, eg repair. This chapter also provides processes, procedures and techniques for generating and forwarding transport related information and also provides processes, procedures and techniques for generating and forwarding invoices as well as for the invoice acceptance or invoice rejection

Chapter 3.3 Performance Based Logistics (PBL); this chapter describes the concept of Performance Based Logistics and its contractual framework. Furthermore, a description of the usage of existing messages, data elements and Key Performance Indicators (KPIs) that can be used to create an individual PBL contract is given.

Chapter 4 Communication Techniques

The purpose of this chapter is to describe how S2000M messages are set up and exchanged using the S2000M XML schema.

Chapter 5 Data Model

The purpose of this chapter is to describe the UML data model that results ultimately in the S2000M XML schema. This data model provides a better comprehension of the data relationships.

Chapter 6 Data Dictionary

The Data Dictionary provides definitions for all data elements used in S2000M. Its purpose is to identify the standardized names, definitions and attributes to ensure a common understanding and application of the data elements.

Chapter 7 Definitions, Abbreviations and Reference Documents

The glossary of terms and definitions is a catalogue of all the terms utilized in S2000M chapters 1 to 6. Its purpose is to identify the terms and explain their definitions to ensure a common understanding of S2000M.

In addition, it provides an overview of all reference documents used in S2000M.

S2000M specification development history

1981

The ASD (former AECMA) supply working group was founded.

1992

Issue 2.1 - The first issue to be used in support of a project.

1998

Issue 3.0 - Introduction of Chap 5 (Repair), SQ1 (Order based pricing), deletion of Appendix 5 (EDIFACT).

2005

Issue 4.0 - Extension to land and sea. Introduction of Chap 6 ("S2000M Light")

2012

Issue 5.0 - Move the repair information (Chap 5) to Chap 3

2015

Issue 6.0, published December 2015, introduced a set of XML messages, based on the long term objective to use established product data standards as the backbone for data exchange. The specification will be supported by the creation of interface specifications for data exchange with other disciplines (S1000D and S3000L).

2017

Issue 6.1 March 2017

2021

Issue 7.0 – Published April 2021. Includes changes related to Data and Export Control or Trade Control and introduction of Performance Based Logistics (PBL) as well as further details on obsolescence and obsolescence management. Harmonization of terminology across the entire S-Series IPS specifications. Modelling of Issue 7.0 follows the Common Data Model (CDM) for the S-Series IPS specifications.

Ten-liner

The specification S2000M defines the processes, procedures and provides the information for data exchange to be used for material management throughout the lifecycle of a product.

Its purpose is to standardize the business relationship between two or more parties (eg contractor and customer) by providing the data elements, the process flow and the relevant transactions for data exchange.

The specification S2000M is organized into the following chapters:

- Chapter 1 Provisioning
- Chapter 2 Spare Parts List
- Chapter 3 Material Supply
- Chapter 4 Communication Techniques
- Chapter 5 Data Model
- Chapter 6 Data Dictionary
- Chapter 7 Definitions, Abbreviations and Reference Documents

Website

Free download is available at www.s2000m.org

7   S3000L - International specification for Logistics Support Analysis - LSA

Introduction

With the introduction of modern complex technical products, a proper support system must be made available in a timely manner. This requires an extended analysis process to ensure consideration of product support requirements during the design of the product and its support system. The process includes a number of analysis activities concerning a wide range of technical and support considerations and the careful documentation of the results of these analysis activities. The achievement of proper supportability is of crucial importance concerning operation and life cycle costs. Early consideration of product support aspects is increasingly important with regard to both operational and economic aspects. A product that cannot be operated and maintained properly and cost effectively is not acceptable to the operator.

Additionally, a support solution must be scrutinized on a regular basis by analyzing operational and cost efficiency. For this purpose, optimization processes are required. In the S-series IPS specifications, those processes are In-Service Support Optimization (ISSO), documented in S3000L, and In-Service Maintenance Optimization (ISMO), documented in S4000P.

Purpose

The S3000L specification is designed to cover the activities and requirements governing the establishment of the LSA process.

S3000L:

- provides rules for the establishment of the product breakdown and for the selection of LSA candidate items to be analyzed in detail
- describes type and methodology of the specified analysis activities
- provides guidelines about how to process the results of analysis activities and on how to achieve a cost-efficient support solution
- provides guidelines on how to identify and describe product support task requirements

- provides guidelines on how to describe a product support task by the means of a Maintenance Task Analysis (MTA)
- provides guidelines how to scrutinize an existing support solution by the means of an ISSO process
- covers the interface to the customer within the LSA process
- covers the interface between the LSA process and the support engineering areas (eg reliability, maintainability and testability)
- covers the interface between the LSA process and other IPS elements, which provide the typical IPS deliverables:
  - personnel and training
  - supply support
  - technical data services
  - special support and test equipment
  - facilities and infrastructure
  - IT support

S3000L specification development history

In 2006, the development work was assigned to an international team of experts working under the joint chairmanship of AIA and ASD representatives. The following companies and organizations contributed to the development of the initial issue:

– Agusta Westland	United Kingdom
– Airbus	Germany
– Boeing	USA
– Dassault Aviation	France
– EADS Casa	Spain
– EADS Military Systems	Germany
– Eurocopter	France
– LOGSA	USA
– MBDA	France
– Saab AB	Sweden
– UK MoD	United Kingdom

The final draft of the specification S3000L (Issue 0.1) was published in June 2009. The main purpose of this draft was to enable experts from interested companies and organizations to provide comments on the first approach to the S3000L expert team. The commenting phase was officially closed by end of 2009.

In June 2010, Issue 1.0 of S3000L was finally released and published for free download via the website of ASD-STAN. With the signing of a Memorandum of Understanding between ASD and AIA at the Farnborough Air Show in July 2010, the IPS Spec Council was formed and the IPS community implemented a new platform for harmonization and coordination of the different S-Series IPS specifications activities. In November 2010 the kickoff of the S3000L Steering Committee (SC) took place in Washington, the first official S3000L SC meeting was conducted in April 2011 in Paris.

Issue 1.1 was published in July 2014. It included an updated UML data model, an updated chapter 10 on Scheduled Maintenance Analysis (harmonized with S4000P) and a completely modified chapter 16 concerning In-service LSA as a continuous process over the complete product life cycle.

Issue 2.0 was published in April 2021 as a part of the 2021 S-Series IPS specifications block release. It includes a major rework of specific chapters, especially the chapters concerning product breakdown (chapter 4) and corrective maintenance analysis (chapter 7). The chapter concerning in-service LSA (now chapter 17) was considerably extended to describe the required steps of an ISSO process in greater detail.

The following issues of S3000L have been published:

- S3000L Issue 1.0: June 2010
- S3000L Issue 1.1: July 2014
- S3000L Issue 2.0: April 2021 (part of 2021 S-Series IPS specifications block release)

Ten-liner

S3000L describes the processes and analysis activities to be used for the definition of a suitable support system, needed to operate technical complex, cost-intensive and long living products. In addition to the extensive procedural chapters in the specification, the corresponding data requirements are described by a detailed data model using UML (Unified Modeling Language). The data model per se is predicated upon ISO 10303:239 Product Life Cycle Support (PLCS).

The specification is organized into 22 chapters, which can be grouped into the following clusters:

- Chapter 1   Introduction and general guidance how to use the specification

- Chapter 2 - 17   Procedural chapters describing LSA process and analysis activities
- Chapter 18   Description of interrelations to other S-Series IPS specifications
- Chapter 19 - 20 Data model and data exchange
- Chapter 21   Terms, abbreviations and acronyms
- Chapter 22   Alphabetical Data Element List (DEL)

Website

Free download is available at www.s3000l.org

8 S4000P - International specification for developing and continuously improving preventive maintenance

Introduction

For a new Supported Product (SP) or for a new SP variant, the maintainability of its intended design must be assessed by maintainability specialists providing engineering support. The results from that assessment must be available during the Design and Development (D&D) phase latest prior to Critical Design Reviews (CDR).

The scope is to develop and justify applicable and effective Preventive Maintenance Task Requirements (PMTR) on an analytical basis and/or to have influence on the design for the SP under analysis in due time. During the analysis activities, inputs from Reliability, Maintainability, Testability and Safety (RMTS) experts are required and in-service experience with other SP and/or with single equipment/items installed on other SP must be taken into account (if available).

According to the overall scope, the specification S4000P must cover all types of SP including any complex technical platform, system, equipment or facility (e.g. on air/sea/land, under the sea-/ground-level, in space).

For an individual analysis project, the S4000P analysis methodologies must be tailored and precisely written in an analysis guideline or Policy and Procedure Handbook (PPH) to be accepted by regulatory authorities (if involved), maintainers, operators, manufacturers, suppliers etc. The released document must allow a structured, traceable and complete determination of all required PMTR, leading to an operator-specific set of preventive maintenance tasks summarized in an Operators' Maintenance Program (OMP) afterwards. During the later in-service phase the SP maintenance program results from these OMP data taking into account operator-specific usage data (refer to S3000L Chapter 10).

In addition to all processes being selected for developing PMTR, S4000P provides additional processes to review and optimize preventive maintenance tasks from a valid maintenance program on the basis of in-service data/experience.

The combination of PMTR development and a later review plus optimization of valid preventive maintenance tasks during the in-service phase is provided by S4000P only. This analysis combination covers the whole SP life cycle, combines the analytical PMTR background with in-service data and keeps the set of preventive maintenance tasks for the SP applicable, effective and up to date. All S4000P-based processes applied allow the full traceability of all decisions with justifications done during the respective analytical work.

Purpose

The primary objective of analysis methodologies based on S4000P Chapter 2 is to assist regulatory authorities (if involved), other bodies being responsible for SP safety, conformity with law and environmental integrity, to achieve customers'/operators' specification data or expectations and to support all parties being involved in the analytical process developing, approving and releasing the identified Preventive Maintenance Task Requirements (PMTR).

PMTR can be subdivided into the following requirements:

- PMTRI: Preventive Maintenance Task Requirements with repetitive scheduled Intervals and
- PMTRE: Preventive Maintenance Task Requirements being applicable after special Events without any repetitive scheduled intervals.

S4000P Issue 2.1 Chapter 2 provides analytical methodologies for developing both PMTRI and PMTRE during the Design and Development (D&D) phase of a SP. These methodologies are also applicable to analyze technical modifications and/or supplements of the design in systems and/or of structure and/or of zones of the SP during later LC phases.

The secondary objective of this specification is to continuously improve preventive maintenance of the SP on basis of analysis methodologies provided in S4000P Chapter 3.For a continuous improvement of all documented preventive maintenance tasks, in-service data/feedback must be taken into account by the responsible analyst(s).

For the review and optimization of a valid SP maintenance program, the In-Service Maintenance Optimization (ISMO) process is applicable. To review and optimize the sets of preventive maintenance tasks, which have to be performed after special events, a different process is defined in S4000P Chapter 3.

Both the initial PMTR development and the subsequent review and improvement of the preventive maintenance tasks must support the achievement of the following aspects:

- Ensure / maintain safety, including safety/emergency systems and/or emergency equipment for the SP,
- Avoid any conflict with law(s) and/or any significant impact on environmental integrity (ecological damage) during mission/operation and/or during maintenance activities,
- Optimize mission/operational capability/availability,
- Optimize economy (reduction of Life Cycle Costs = LCC).

For individual analysis projects either all of the above listed aspects or only a limited set of these aspects can be selected to be analysis-relevant according to the project-specific analysis guideline/PPH.

S4000P main advantages and innovations:

- In comparison to other known analytical methodologies, the application of S4000P is not limited to pre-selected SP types like military and/or civil aircraft for example. All S4000P analytical principles are developed by industry to be applicable for all complex technical SP. This comprises SP operating in the air, on the ground, under the ground, floating, submerged or even in space for civil and/or military usage.
- S4000P is an integrated part of the S-Series IPS specifications and ensures effective data generation and data exchange with the other S-Series IPS specifications, customers, responsible authority(s)(if involved), design departments, suppliers, supportability departments etc. to enable an effective and integrated Customer support and IPS. To enable a dynamic data exchange in-between the S-Series IPS specifications and with external parties in the future, the S4000P data model will be provided in Chapter 5 in next document issues.
- The application of S4000P ensures development and continuous improvement to a balanced and effective preventive maintenance regime for the SP, which also results in a reduction of corrective maintenance effort.

- To cover the whole life cycle of a SP, S4000P is not limited on an initial development of PMTRI and PMTRE during the design and development phase of a SP only (see Chapter 2). It provides additional processes to continuously improve the set of preventive maintenance tasks with repetitive scheduled intervals (see Chapter 3).
- When defining PMTRI for SP systems on basis of Chapter 2, S4000P synergizes identified PMTRI with maintenance tasks being defined on the basis of integrated test- and condition monitoring technology being realized more often in future and modern SP.
- When defining PMTRI for the SP structure according to S4000P Chapter 2, identified maintenance task requirements are synergized with the integrated structure condition monitoring technology.
- S4000P covers the analysis of all kinds of present and future structural materials and material combinations.
- A modular and flexible analysis concept enables a zonal analysis of all types of SP to define PMTRI for its zones in S4000P Chapter 2.
- Information concerning the consolidation and harmonization of different PMTRI resulting from system-, structure- , zonal analysis and other task requirements (if any) is provided in S4000P Chapter 2.
- In addition to PMTRI development S4000P Chapter 2 contains a process for the initial development of PMTRE selected for special events impacting a SP.
- S4000P Chapter 3 describes the ISMO process to optimize PMTRI and consequently, the resulting preventive maintenance tasks with repetitive scheduled intervals in the valid documentation of the SP.
- S4000P Chapter 3 is completed with a process applicable for the in-service review, including an optimization of PMTRE.
- The contents of Chapters 4 to 7 is described in the "Ten-Liner" (see below)
- S4000P contains analysis examples and examples for PPH contents in Chapter 7

Note:

NATO has recommended the ISMO process of S4000P Issue 1.0 Chapter 3 in 2017 on the basis of the document NATO STANREC 4795. The ISMO process from Issue 1.0

remains unchanged in Chapter 3 of Issue 2.0 and in this Issue 2.1.

S4000P specification development history and update process

The initial S4000P development work started in 2013 on the basis of several draft specification versions. The first publication of S4000P Issue 1.0 took place in May 2014. Issue 2.0 was published in August 2018 and Issue 2.1 was published in conjunction with the first bloc release of the S-Series IPS specifications.

For the published document Issues 1.0, 2.0 and 2.1, the S4000P working groups have been composed of European experts from the following international companies and authorities:

–	AIRBUS Defence & Space	Germany & Spain
–	AIRBUS Helicopters	Germany
–	Babcock International Group (LSC Group)	UK
–	BAE Systems	United Kingdom
–	DBM Engineering Solutions Ltd	United Kingdom
–	Fox Flight Systems	Germany
–	HICO-ICS GmbH t/a HICO Technology Austria (HICO-AT)	Austria
–	Isselnord S.R.L.	Italy
–	Logistikkommando der Bundeswehr	Germany
–	Saab AB	Sweden
–	Sopra Steria	France/Germany
–	thyssenkrupp Marine Systems (tkMS)	United Kingdom
–	UK MoD	United Kingdom

Note:

The US Company O'Neil & Associates, Inc. (USA) has always supported the S4000P Steering Committee (SC), including all S4000P working groups, in the frame of the editorial work prior to the publication of specification issues 1.0, 2.0 and 2.1. For future specification issues an involvement of AIA industry members is planned and expected to form a combined ASD/AIA team instead of the current ASD team.

Ten-liner

The specification S4000P Issue 2.1 defines processes and procedures as well as providing information and examples how to develop and continuously improve Preventive Maintenance Task Requirements (PMTR) specific for technical complex SP during a SP life cycle. Its purpose is to contribute to the SP safety, to ensure conformity with law(s) and regulations including environmental integrity, to achieve maximum mission/operational availability and to minimize operational and maintenance costs during the SP life cycle.

The specification S4000P Issue 2.1 contains the following chapters:

- Chapter 1   Introduction to the specification
- Chapter 2   Developing PMTR
- Chapter 3   Optimizing PMTR
- Chapter 4   S4000P Interfaces
- Chapter 5   Data model and data exchange
- Chapter 6   Terms, abbreviations and acronyms
- Chapter 7   Examples

Note:
Until the latest document Issue 2.1, the S4000P data model is not yet included in Chapter 5. However the next issue of the specification will provide it.

Website

Free download of S4000P is available at www.s4000p.org

9   S5000F - International specification for in-service data feedback

Introduction

In-service data feedback is one of the most important functions in-service support. It enables fleet managers, support managers and manufacturers to perform a thorough analysis of operational and maintenance performance of a complex technical system.

The results of the analysis can be the basis for:

- enhancement of the maintenance and support concept
- improvement of the product or the system by modifications and retrofit activities
- on-condition maintenance
- refined operational planning
- management of requirements and contracts
- provision of sophisticated (traditional or digital) services

The overall aim to be achieved through in-service data feedback is the increase of fleet availability and optimization of the support and product effectiveness, as well as to provide reporting capabilities to both customers and authorities. In addition, the in-service data feedback information is a firm requirement by industry to agree to and manage in-service contracts and to fulfil their obligations in regard to product liability.

The scope of S5000F is to handle information which is to be exchanged between different stakeholders during the in-service phase. The specification does not only cover information from the operator to the industry or maintainer but also information from the industry or maintainer to the operator or third parties such as involved authorities. The information can be exchanged in any direction, as the direction of the exchange for a same dataset might vary based on the contractual in-service support arrangements. The exchange can be also within internal systems.

The processes in the specification focus on operational and maintenance feedback information and the activities that take place in the operational phases of the life cycle of the product. The life cycle of a product is divided as per SX000i into five phases:

- preparation

- development
- production
- in-service
- disposal

The last two phases, in-service and disposal, are the phases that are mainly handled within the scope of S5000F. This does not preclude using S5000F during other product phases, eg, to provide information about a legacy program during the concept phase, or to provide feedback about operational tests. It is also known that S5000F is used to exchange quality assurance data for a manufacturing program.

The in-service data feedback information is transferred to the organization of interest using a data model that is consistent with SX002D. The actual exchange is performed using XML messages.

Purpose

The purpose of using S5000F alone or together with the other S-Series IPS specifications is to obtain a structured way to handle the in-service (including operational and maintenance) data feedback between different stakeholders. Stakeholders can be operators, industries (manufacturers or maintainers), vendors, suppliers, authorities, etc.

By using the data model of S5000F and its associated XML schemas for actual data exchange, this purpose can be achieved in a standard and efficient way.

S5000F specification development history

During 2008 the plans for developing the S5000F were drawn up by the AIA/ASD IPS Spec Council. There were already some S-Series IPS specifications developed and used for integrated product support purposes.

The IPS Spec Council noted that there was a need for a specification handling operational and maintenance data feedback from the operational field or the in-service field to the maintainer and/or the product manufacturer.

It was decided that the S5000F specification had to:

- take into account the activity model given by ISO 10303-239 PLCS and support data exchange on PLCS-based data exchange sets

- include process application guidelines and rules for information exchange
- be tailorable and include guidelines for tailoring
- take into account current ISO/EN baseline documents
- enable online interfaces to the S-Series IPS specifications, ie S1000D, S2000M, S3000L, S4000P, and the (then) future S6000T and SX000i

The kick off meeting was held in Munich in October 2008. At this meeting the purpose and the scope of S5000F were presented for interested industries and organizations (eg, armed forces and authorities).

The development work was allocated to an international team of experts working under the joint chairmanship of ASD and AIA representatives. At a certain moment in time, the team agreed that S5000F would require to cover much more than just operations and maintenance, and the title was changed to cover the whole in-service phase. The following companies/organizations have contributed or are currently contributing to the development:

– Airbus Defence & Space	Germany/Spain
– Airbus Helicopters	France/Germany
– Andromeda Systems Inc.	USA
– Atkins Global	United Kingdom
– Boeing	USA
– Bundeswehr	Germany
– Cimpa	France
– Dassault Aviation	France
– Dutch MoD	Netherlands
– ESG	Germany
– GE Aviation	USA
– Leonardo	Italy
– Nexter Group	France
– NH Industries	France
– OCCAR	Europe
– O'Neil & Associates, Inc.	USA
– Rolls-Royce	UK
– Saab	Sweden
– Shipdex	(international consortium for the shipping industry, based in Italy)
– UK MoD	United Kingdom

Note

Though initially S5000F was supposed to be PLCS-based, the non-availability of PLCS tools and the development of the S-Series Common Data Model (SX002D) redirected the development towards the common XML-base messages used by the S-Series IPS specifications. Mapping to PLCS Edition 3 is ongoing.

Issue 1.0 was published in September 2016.

Issue 2.0 was published in December 2019.

Issue 3.0 was published in April 2021, as part of the 2021 S-Series IPS specifications block release.

Ten-liner

S5000F - International specification for in-service data feedback describes a structured way to share information between different stakeholders regarding a product or service during the in-service phase. The information is transferred using an XML schema that is interoperable with the other S-Series IPS specifications. The exchange is multidirectional, and the direction may vary depending on contractual arrangements.

Collection of in-service data has many purposes and is one of the most important functions of in-service support. It enables fleet managers, support managers and manufacturers to perform a thorough analysis of the operational and support performance of a complex product and organize complex services; it also allows authorities to confirm that adherence to current regulations is complied with.

The overall aim to be achieved through in-service data feedback is the increase of fleet availability and optimization of support and product effectiveness. In addition, the in-service data feedback information is a firm requirement by Industry to agree to and manage in-service contracts and to fulfill their obligations with regard to product liability.

Website

Free download is available at www.s5000f.org

10 S6000T - International specification for training analysis and design

Introduction

Today's technical products are more complex with increasing capabilities, the need to train users and maintainers has become a huge challenge. Budgets have grown tighter increasing the pressure to identify what to train and how to train it. S6000T, International specification for training analysis and design, provides a structured methodology for determining those requirements and identifying the key data points to clearly communicate these training requirements.

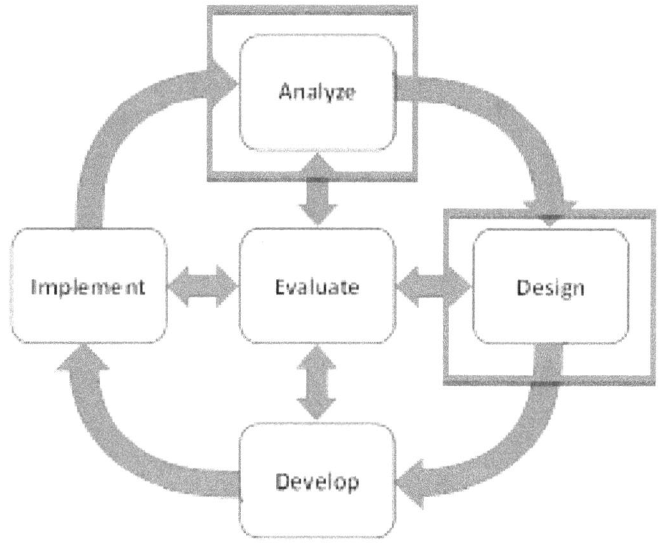

ICN-S6000T-B6865-00001-001-01

Fig 3 ADDIE model

The Instructional Systems Development (ISD) process is comprised of five interrelated phases that are often referred to as the "ADDIE" model: Analyze, Design, Develop, Implement, and Evaluate. S6000T scope includes the first 2 phases in the process; Analyze and Design. S6000T is the latest S-Series IPS specification being drafted by ASD/AIA with the purpose of standardizing the process and data developed by different organizations.

S6000T defines the process for performing a Training Needs Analysis (TNA), including the definition of training requirements, learning objectives, and the identification of training curriculum. It also identifies the data model for information exchange with other S-Series IPS specifications.

Purpose

The S6000T – International specification for training analysis and design supports the definition of all levels of requirements and design data necessary to support product training.

S6000T:

- Provides guidelines for gathering information when performing a training analysis
- Provides methodologies and key business objects during the analysis phase including:
    - Performing a training situation analysis
    - Performing a mission, job, task analysis
    - Identifying task prioritization for training
    - Performing training task analysis
    - Developing training strategies.

- Provides methodologies and key business objects collected during the design phase including;
    - Identifying training target audience
    - Identifying learning gaps
    - Developing learning objectives
    - Defining an assessment strategy
    - Defining an instructional strategy
    - Performing a media selection
    - Sequencing learning objectives
    - Identifying training system alternatives
    - Determine training system requirements
    - Developing a curriculum outline

- Provides a comprehensive data model for the Analysis and Design phases
- Provides a methodology for optimizing in-service performance optimization

S6000T specification development

The following companies/organizations contributed to the development of the first two issues of S6000T:

–	Airbus Defence and Space	Germany
–	Aloft AeroArchitects	USA
–	BNH	Canada
–	Boeing	USA
–	Bundeswehr	Germany
–	Collins Aerospace	United Kingdom
–	EPS Corporation	USA
–	ISS	USA
–	LGM	Belgium
–	O'Neil & Associates, Inc.	USA
–	Saab	Sweden
–	UK MoD	United Kingdom
–	US Navy	USA

Issue 1.0 was published March 2020

Issue 2.0 was published in September 2021, as part of the 2021 S-Series IPS specifications block release.

Ten-liner

S6000T defines the process and data needed to support the implementation of the analyze and design phase of the Instructional System Design (ISD) based on the Analyze, Design, Develop, Implement and Evaluate (ADDIE) paradigm.

S6000T Issue 2.0 defines the process and procedures and underlying data model for performing training analysis and design activities.

The specification S6000T Issue 2.0 contains the following chapters:

–	Chapter 1	Introduction to the specification
–	Chapter 2	Information gathering
–	Chapter 3	Analysis
–	Chapter 4	Design
–	Chapter 5	In Service Human Performance
–	Chapter 6	Relationship to other specifications
–	Chapter 7	Data model
–	Chapter 8	Terms, abbreviations and acronyms

Website

Free download is available at www.s6000t.org

Page intentionally blank

11   SX001G - Glossary for the S-Series IPS specifications

Introduction

Interoperability between the respective S-Series IPS specifications requires a common terminology to be applied to all the specifications. The SX001G Glossary contains terms and definitions as well as acronyms used in the S-Series IPS specifications and guides users towards a common terminology. The task of developing a consolidated and harmonized common terminology across the S-Series IPS specifications is very large and requires the collaboration of a number of individual groups. The Data Modeling and Exchange Working Group (DMEWG) is responsible for coordinating the development and publication, the Terminology Working Group (TWG) is responsible for the consolidation and harmonization of terms and definitions, and the IPS Spec Council and the respective S-Series IPS specifications Steering Committees are responsible for review, acceptance, and incorporation of the terms and definitions.

Purpose

The purpose of SX001G is to manage:

- definitions for central business terms used in the S-Series IPS specifications
- definitions for all terms used in the S-Series IPS specifications data models
- approved abbreviations and acronyms which can be used in the respective S-Series IPS specifications and/or in the naming of terms within the S-Series IPS specifications data models.

The DMEWG provides rules and guidelines for SX001G including:

- naming conventions
- authoring of definitions for the dictionary
- metadata required for each term
- relationship between S-Series IPS specifications terminology and OASIS PLCS Reference data

SX001G specification development

The development work was initiated in 2011. The following companies and organizations contribute to the work:

–	Airbus Defence & Space	Spain
–	Boeing	USA
–	ISS	USA
–	LOGSA	USA
–	Nexter Group	France
–	O'Neil & Associates, Inc.	USA
–	Pentecom	USA
–	Rolls-Royce	United Kingdom
–	Saab AB	Sweden

Issue 1.0 was published in December 2014.

Issue 1.1 was published in August 2015.

Issue 2.0 was published in December 2018.

Issue 3.0 was published in April 2021 as part of the 2021 S-Series IPS specifications block release.

Ten-liner

SX001G – Glossary for the S-Series IPS specifications includes the terms and definitions that are essential for understanding the central concepts and information defined in the S-Series IPS specifications. The Glossary includes central business terms and definitions, the data model terms and definitions, and abbreviations and acronyms. Rules and guidelines for the authoring of SX001G (eg, naming conventions, definition writing rules) are maintained by the Data Modeling and Exchange Working Group.

In the past, the respective S-Series IPS specifications have not collaborated consistently on terminology. The establishment of the Glossary will not only help specification users, but will serve as a forcing function to harmonize terminology across the set of S-Series IPS specifications.

Website

Free download is available at www.sx000i.org.

12 SX002D - Common data model for the S-Series IPS specifications

Introduction

Interoperability between the respective S-Series IPS specifications requires a common understanding of the key concepts to be applied to all the specifications. The SX002D Common Data Model (CDM) is a conceptual description of all data elements common to more than one S-Series IPS specification. The task of developing a consolidated and harmonized data model across the S-Series IPS specifications is very large and requires the collaboration of a number of individual groups. The Data Modeling and Exchange Working Group (DMEWG) is responsible for coordinating the development and publication.

Purpose

The purpose of SX002D is to harmonize data modeling activities that are performed within each individual S-Series IPS specification, and to consolidate data requirements into one coherent S-Series data model, using UML.

SX002D lays out the harmonized end-state common terminology/model for all S-Series IPS specifications and aims to allow each individual specification to utilize or extend it as needed.

SX002D specification development

The development work was initiated in 2011. The following companies and organizations contribute to the work:

–	Airbus Defence & Space	Spain
–	Boeing	USA
–	ISS	USA
–	Isselnord	Italy
–	LOGSA	USA
–	Nexter Group	France
–	O'Neil & Associates, Inc.	USA
–	Rolls-Royce	United Kingdom
–	Saab AB	Sweden

Issue 1.0 was published in December 2014.

Issue 1.1 was published in August 2015.

Issue 2.0 was published in December 2018.

Issue 2.1 was published in April 2021 as part of the 2021 S-Series IPS specifications block release.

Ten-liner

SX002D – Common data model for the S-Series IPS specifications includes a conceptual description of all data elements common to more than one S-Series IPS specification, and documents this as a consolidated and harmonized data model using UML.

Definitions for all classes and attributes defined in the SX002D Common Data Model are published as part of SX001G Glossary for the S-Series IPS specifications.

In the past, the respective S-Series IPS specifications have not collaborated consistently on concepts and terminology. The establishment of the Common Data Model will not only help specification users, but will serve as a forcing function to harmonize concepts and terminology across the set of S-Series IPS specifications.

Website

Free download is available at www.sx000i.org.

13   SX004G - UML model reader's guide

Introduction

A central part for future issues of the S-Series IPS specifications is the definition of a data model which defines data needed for performing and for sharing the outcome of the processes described in the respective S-Series IPS specifications. These data models must be documented using Unified Modeling Language (UML) class models as mandated by the DMEWG.

In order to avoid that each S-Series IPS specifications have to include instructions for the readers on how to read and understand a UML class model the IPS Spec Council decided to publish a separate specification for this matter, which then can be referenced from the respective specification.

Purpose

The SX004G UML readers' guide is a document describing how to read and understand the UML class models created for any given S-Series IPS specification, including the common data model (SX002D).

Issue 1.0 was published in August 2016.

Issue 2.0 was published in April 2021 as part of the 2021 S-Series IPS specifications block release.

SX004G specification development

The development work was initiated in 2014. The following companies and organizations contribute to the work:

–	Airbus Defense & Space	Spain
–	Boeing	USA
–	HiCo	Austria
–	ISS	USA
–	Isselnord	Italy
–	KCIG	Germany
–	Nexter Group	France
–	O'Neil & Associates, Inc.	USA
–	Saab AB	Sweden

Website

Free download is available at www.sx000i.org.

14 SX005G - S-Series IPS specifications XML schema implementation guide

Introduction

The S-Series IPS specifications provide XML schemas to support interoperability between the different S-Series IPS specifications, as well as to support data exchange between its defined business processes and external stakeholders.

In order to implement and use XML schemas which are developed in accordance with the guidelines from the DMEWG (all specifications but S1000D) the SX005G gives further details needed to support software developers.

Purpose

The purpose of the XML implementation guidance is to provide clear instruction on how to use and implement the S-Series IPS specifications XML Schemas to support data exchange, and to ensure that all parties have a common understanding on the principles behind.

Issue 1.0 was published in December 2017.

Issue 2.0 was published in April 2021 as part of the 2021 S-Series IPS specifications block release.

SX005G specification development

The development work was initiated in 2014. The following companies and organizations contribute to the work:

–	Airbus Defense & Space	Spain
–	Boeing	USA
–	ISS	USA
–	Isselnord	Italy
–	KCIG	Germany
–	Nexter Group	France
–	Defense & Space	USA
–	Saab AB	Sweden

Website

Free download is available at www.sx000i.org.

15 SX006R - S-Series IPS specifications rules definition guide

Introduction

The processes, data models and use cases of the S-Series IPS specifications cover the most common and significant requirements of their users. However, in some cases, tailoring of the specifications may be required. Part of this tailoring is performed by answering certain decision points that lead to the implementation of business rules.

This specification will support the tailoring of the S-Series IPS specifications by providing guidance for the creation, documentation and implementation of business rules, as well as the exchange between the involved parties.

Such rules could enable, for example, the application (or not) of certain activities, the minimum or maximum length of a field, a conditional cardinality, the use of specific valid values, etc. The definition of the decision points for such rules would be defined in the corresponding specification.

Purpose

SX006R will specify the entire lifecycle of business rules, from their definition and documentation, to their exchange with another party, to their execution.

Issue 1.0 is planned to be published in 2023 as part of the 2023 S-Series IPS specifications block release.

Website

Free download will be available at www.sx000i.org.

16 S1000X, S2000X, S3000X, S4000X, S6000X - Input data specifications

Introduction

S1000X, S2000X, S3000X, S4000X and S6000X will become international specifications that define the input data required by S1000D, S2000M, S3000L, S4000P and S6000T, respectively.

The title of S1000X is for example "Input data specification for S1000D".

The Sn000X specifications (where "n" is a digit) will give rules and guidance for the mapping of elements and attributes from the source data model/schema to the target data model/schema based on the glossary SX001G and the common data model SX002D. The source and target functionality and data schema requirements will be uniquely identified.

The data provided by a source system can have a related "triggering event" for availability. Thus, Sn000X must also include some kind of process description. In addition, the order of data receipt from the different source specifications/systems can be important. In this case, the order relationship and interdependence of the data must also be defined in the mapping requirements. If necessary, differing terms between the source and target with same meaning need also to be mapped in the respective input data specification.

Note that neither S5000F nor SX000i have an input data specification associated with them because their outputs have the same format at their inputs and no special mapping is required from other specifications. Source information for these two specifications will come from a variety of tools, but not from other S-Series IPS specifications.

Purpose

The purpose of S1000X, S2000X, S3000X, S4000X and S6000X is to specify all input data required from other specifications to S1000D, S2000M, S3000L, S4000P and S6000T, respectively, in a standardized way. The definition of these required input data is not limited to the S-Series IPS specifications but must include any source necessary to create the respective deliverables.

The use of the Sn000X specifications is not essential to the use of the master specifications, but it is an important aid for the implementation of IT systems that are compliant with the S-Series of IPS specifications, as these will define the interfaces for such IT systems.

S1000X specification development

The development work for S1000X was initiated in October 2014.

The following companies and organizations contribute to the S1000X work:

–	Airbus Defence & Space	Germany
–	Airbus Helicopters	Germany
–	BAE Systems	United Kingdom
–	Defense & Space	USA
–	Dutch MoD	Netherlands
–	FBC	Austria
–	Finmeccanica	Italy
–	ISS	USA
–	Isselnord	Italy
–	NAVSEA/DoD	USA
–	NSPA/NATO	Luxemburg
–	Saab	Sweden

Issue 1.0 of S1000X is planned to be published by end of 2021 and will cover the required input data for S1000D 4.1 from S2000M 6.1, S3000L 1.1 and from GEIA-STD-0007 Revision B.

Free download will be available at www.s1000d.org as well as at www.sx000i.org

S2000X specification development

The start of S2000X had to wait until the complete S2000M data model was available. Once S2000M Issue 7.0 has been published, the work of S2000X has been initiated by the S2000M SC and is expected to finalize with the next block release.

Free download will be available at www.s2000m.org/.

S3000X specification development

The development work for S3000X was initiated in April 2018 by the S3000L SC.

The task team is composed of members of the S3000L SC, each acting as a point of contact to the other ASD specifications.

Issue 1.0 of S3000X is planned to cover input data mapping from S1000D, S2000M, S4000P, S5000F, S6000T and SX000i to S3000L.

The following companies and organizations contribute to the S3000X work:

–	Boeing	UK/USA
–	HICO	Austria
–	Leonardo	Italy

–	Saab	Sweden
–	tkMS	Germany

Free download will be available at www.s3000l.org.

S4000X specification development

S4000X will be developed as soon as the S4000P data model is finalized and is expected to be released at the same time as the 2023 S-Series IPS specifications block release.

Free download will be available at www.s4000p.org.

S6000X specification development

The development work for S6000X was initiated in April 2020 by the S6000T SC.

Issue 1.0 of S6000X is planned to define how support analysis data in the format of S3000L issue 2.0 and SAE-GEIA-STD-0007 Rev C can be used as input data for steps and activities defined in S6000T issue 2.0 Chapter 3 'Training Analysis' and Chapter 4 'Training Design', respectively.

S6000X Issue 1.0 is expected to be available by the end of 2021.

The following companies and organizations contribute to the S6000X work:

–	Boeing	USA
–	ISS	Austria
–	O'Neil & Associates, Inc.	USA
–	Saab	Sweden
–	US Navy	USA

Free download will be available at www.s6000t.org.

Ten-liner

- Sn000X defines all required input data for the respective specification in a standardized way.
- The source and target functionality and data schema requirements are uniquely identified.
- Sn000X gives rules and guidance for the mapping of elements and attributes.
- This includes process descriptions concerning the order of data receipt from the different source specifications/systems including associated triggers.

- The order relationship and interdependence of the data are defined in the mapping requirements.
- The terminology is based on the glossary given in SX001G.
- The source and target data model/schema is based on the common data model in SX002D.
- Schemas are provided to support the transfer of information from the source systems.
- To assist implementations in different projects and/or organizations, business rules and business rule decision points are also provided.

Website

Free downloads of S1000X, S2000X, S3000X, S4000X and S6000X are planned to be available at www.s1000d.org/www.sx000i.org, www.s2000m.org, www.s3000l.org, www.s4000p.org and www.s6000t.org, respectively.

Page intentionally blank

17   ASD-STE100® - Simplified Technical English

Introduction

ASD-STE100® (European Community Trade Mark No. 017966390) is an **International specification for the preparation of technical documentation in a controlled language**. A controlled language is a natural language with special restrictions on grammar, style, and vocabulary usage.

ASD-STE100 (STE) was developed to help the readers of English-language documentation to understand what they read, particularly when these readers are non-native English speakers. Today, the success of STE is such that other industries use it beyond its original intended purpose of aerospace maintenance documentation. Interest in STE has also increased dramatically in the areas of language services, professional translation and interpreting, as well as in the academic world.

Purpose

The purpose of STE is to tell technical writers how to write technical texts in a clear, simple, and unambiguous manner that readers throughout the world will find easy to understand.

The major benefits of adopting STE are:

- Operation and maintenance optimization: controlled grammatical structures and vocabulary - on which STE is based - have the purpose of producing texts that are easily understandable and, consequently, can reduce human errors and improve safety.
- Wide applicability: although STE was originally designed for the aviation industry, it can be used in other areas, such as land and sea vehicles, as detailed in S1000D. In addition, STE can also be used in other industries (for example, power generation, automotive, medical and healthcare, and many others) as well as in the academic world.

STE specification development history

In the late 1970s, the Association of European Airlines (AEA) asked the European Association of Aerospace Industries (AECMA, now ASD) to investigate the readability of maintenance documentation in the civil aviation industry. AECMA asked the

Aerospace Industries Association (AIA) of America to help with this project.

STE development work started in 1983.

The specification was first released in 1986 as the AECMA Simplified English Guide, which, in 2005, became the ASD-STE100 specification. Subsequently, several changes, issues and revisions were released up to the present Issue 8. The specification is fully owned by ASD, Brussels, Belgium. As such, STE is not a part of the S-Series IPS specifications but fully supports them.

The STE specification is maintained by the ASD Simplified Technical English Maintenance Group (STEMG.) The group consists mostly of representatives from ASD countries but there are also representatives from countries that are not members of ASD. The STEMG reports to the ASD Product Support Specification Group (PSSG).

Ten-liner

STE is a set of writing rules (part 1) and a dictionary of controlled vocabulary (part 2).

The writing rules cover aspects of grammar and style. The dictionary gives the general words that a writer can use. There are 53 writing rules in STE included in nine sections:

- Section 1 - Words (14 rules)
- Section 2 - Noun clusters (3 rules)
- Section 3 - Verbs (7 rules)
- Section 4 - Sentences (4 rules)
- Section 5 - Procedural writing (5 rules)
- Section 6 - Descriptive writing (6 rules)
- Section 7 - Safety instructions (3 rules)
- Section 8 - Punctuation and word counts (7 rules)
- Section 9 - Writing practices (4 rules)

The STE controlled general dictionary gives the words that are most frequently used in technical writing. The approved words (approximately 850) were selected because they were simple and easy to recognize.

In addition to the general dictionary, STE permits the use of company-specific or project-oriented technical words (referred to in STE as technical names and technical verbs). These words are referred to the categories listed in the respective rules.

The current specification is Issue 8, dated 30 April 2021. The next Issue 9 will be released in April 2023.

Website

Free copies can be requested at http://www.asd-ste100.org/request.html or downloaded at https://asd-stan.org/downloads/asd-ste100-004/

Page intentionally blank

18 Abbreviations and acronyms

Table 2 Abbreviations and acronyms

Abbreviation	Definition
ADDIE	Analyze, Design, Develop, Implement, and Evaluate
ADL	Advanced Distributed Learning
AECMA	European Association of Aerospace Industries
AIA	Aerospace Industries Association
ASD	Aerospace and Defence Industries Association of Europe
ATA	Air Transport Association
BR	Business Rules
BREX	Business Rules EXchange
CDM	Common Data Model
CDR	Critical Design Reviews
CIR	Common Information Repository
CSDB	Common Source DataBase
D&D	Design and Development
DEL	Data Element List
DMEWG	Data Model and Exchange Working Group
DTD	Document Type Definition
ECA	European Combat Aircraft
EDIFACT	Electronic Data Interchange for Administration, Commerce and Transport
ICN	Information Control Number
IETP	Interactive Electronic Technical Publications
ILS	Integrated Logistics Support (refer to IPS)
IPC	Illustrated Parts Catalogues

IPD	Illustrated Parts Data
IPDP	Illustrated Parts Data Publication
IPS	Integrated Product Support
ISMO	In-Service Maintenance Optimization
ISO	International Standards Organization
ISSO	In-Service Support Optimization
KPI	Key Performance Indicator
LSA	Logistics Support Analysis
MAC	Maintenance Allocation Chart
MoU	Memorandum of Understanding
MTA	Maintenance Task Analysis
NATO	North Atlantic Treaty Organization
NCB	National Codification Bureau
OMP	Operators' Maintenance Program
PBL	Performance Based Logistics
PLCS	Product Life Cycle Support
PMTR	Preventive Maintenance Task Requirements
PMTRE	Preventive Maintenance Task Requirements being applicable after special Events without any repetitive scheduled intervals
PMTRI	Preventive Maintenance Task Requirements with repetitive scheduled Intervals
PPH	Policy and Procedure Handbook
PSSG	Product Support Specification Group
SC	Steering Committee
SCO	Sharable Content Object
SCORM	Sharable Content Object Reference Model
SGML	Standard Generalized Markup Language

SNS	Standard Numbering System
SP	Supported Product
STANREC	STANdards RECommendation
STE	Simplified Technical English
STEMG	Simplified Technical English Management Group
TIR	Technical Information Repository
TNA	Training Needs Analysis
TT	Task Team
TWG	Terminology Working Group
UML	Unified Modeling Language
W3C	World Wide Web Consortium
WG	Working Group

Check out the different specifications in hardcopy:

SX000H, *Handbook for the S-Series Integrated Product Support (IPS) Specifications*, Issue 1.0, ISBN 978-84-19125-18-7

SX000i, *International specification for integrated product support (IPS)*, Issue 3.0, ISBN 978-84-19125-19-4

S1000D, *International specification for technical publications using a common source database,* Issue 5.0, (3 volumes), ISBN 978-84-19125-31-6, 978-84-19125-32-3 and 978-84-19125-33-0

S2000M, *International specification for material management - Integrated data processing* Issue 7.0, ISBN 978-84-19125-29-3

S3000L, *International specification for Logistics Support Analysis – LSA*, Issue 2.0, ISBN 978-84-19125-20-0

S4000P, *International specification for developing and continuously improving preventive maintenance*, Issue 2.1, ISBN 978-84-19125-21-7

S5000F, *International specification for in-service data feedback,* Issue 3.0 (2 volumes), ISBNs 978-84-19125-27-9 & 978-84-19125-28-6

S6000, *International specification for training analysis and design*, Issue 2.0, ISBN 978-84-19125-22-4

SX001G, *Glossary for the S-Series IPS specifications*, Issue 3.0, ISBN 978-84-19125-23-1

SX002D, *Common data model for the S-Series IPS specifications*, Issue 2.1, ISBN 978-84-19125-24-8

SX004G, *UML model reader's guide*, Issue 2.0, ISBN 978-84-19125-25-5

SX005G, *S-Series IPS specifications XML schema implementation guide*, Issue 2.0, ISBN 978-84-19125-26-2

Further books on the S-Series to be published by Editorial Dragon:

An introduction to the S-Series IPS specifications by Ramón Somoza, ISBN 978-84-19125-16-3

S-Series data models and XML schemas by Ramón Somoza, ISBN 978-84-19125-17-0